LIGHTNING
The Nature of Leadership

LIGHTNING
The Nature of Leadership

by Bob Scher

with photographs by Jane English

CODHILL PRESS   NEW PALTZ   NEW YORK

Dedicated
to
the Heron and the Owl

Published in 2003 by
Codhill Press
www.codhill.com

Cover design by Jane English
Page design by Bob Scher

Library of Congress Cataloging-in-Publication Data
Scher, Bob
Lightning: the nature of leadership / by Bob Scher; with photographs by Jane English.
p.cm.
ISBN 1-930337-09-4 (alk.paper)
1. Leadership—Poetry. I. Title
PS3619.C349 L5 2003
811'.6—dc21

Printed in the U.S.A.

"Know the right moment."

Pittacus, c. 600 B.C.

"The stuff of the universe, woven in a single piece according to one and the same system, but never repeating itself...represents a single figure..."

Pierre Teilhard de Chardin

"Your character is your fate."

Heraclitus

CONTENTS

FOLLOWING

Leadership
is also about
following

to pursue a course
whose charts are indistinct
whose way is streaked with turbulence
reveals one's vulnerabilities

that is why true leaders
regardless of
their public show
know what they lack

COMMON-SENSE APPROACH

In many situations
high-minded
revolutionary methods
won't work

For instance
no matter how forceful
or oblique
management is

without it
natural processes
go haywire

LIGHTNING

When things look bad
and everyone is grumbling

when economic conditions
are worsening

when both inside and out
are unsettled

when even the weather
is awful

opportunity
strikes

PATHS

The skill of management
lies at the center
of life
managing the waywardness
of kitchen crumbs

The art of management
may seem different
but goes deep to
the same
core

Whatever the approach
the primary impediment may be
not knowing how
to manage
oneself

LEARNING IN LIFE

In relationships
weaknesses count the most

as each of us struggles
we can begin to appreciate
the other's difficulty

In business
strengths are more important

if someone executes well
someone else
will take up the slack

LEADING

Attentiveness to others
builds loyalty

Inner resolve
gives weight

Vision
yields purpose

if you are missing
the first
you encourage
the unreliable

if you are missing
the second
you are subject
to betrayal

if you are missing
the last
you are missing
the point

NOTHING NEW HERE

These principles
are ingrained

the more in accord
we are

the more effective
and translucent

our personal
style

GIFTS

When a gift comes to you
it is discourteous
and unfortunate
to refuse it

If it conceals deadly arrows
or dangling strings
then the best movement
is an extremely courteous
sidestep

NEW PHYSICS

Money is not what you think
not tokens coin or gold
not material
that can be touched

Like electricity
when current flows through the wire
it surrounds the players
like a field

In every kingdom
money is neither made nor lost
Utterly passive

it is attracted along
invisible paths
by a deeper gravity

POSITION

To be first
is special
whether laurels descend
or not

To be first
is dangerous
the succeeding champion
may learn from your mistakes

Not to be first
may also be the true
path to follow

What to do?

POSITIONING

There is no law against
emphasizing
your own best features

But do not stray so far from yourself
that you forget
your own exaggerations

CHOICE

Life is a business
does this shock you

Getting and spending
our interior forces

to what aim

Better ponder
since guess what

If you choose the wrong one
you will not be permitted

to take it with you

EXERCISE IN NON-JUDGMENT

If it rains
you can open your umbrella
put on your raincoat
or run around nearly naked
and get
soaked

Or
you can lock your door
crawl into bed
and sleep soundly
until everything is
just perfect

MAKING AN APPEARANCE

The time arrives when
appearances are paramount
How we present ourselves

is one responsibility
we cannot avoid

for even carelessness
or indifference
is a presentation

MOVING BEYOND

Who ponders hastily
moves ill

Who ponders wearily
moves clumsily

Who ponders deliberately
moves well

and no matter what the outcome
has no regrets

RESULTS

Boldness
without vision
gives stupid results

vision
without boldness
gives no results

boldness combined
with vision
is a promising start

Unless you imagine
that success
will resolve

your fundamental
difficulties

SPEAKING

There are three principles
of communication

The first is
unmistakable
clarity

resist cluttering your speech
with too many
notions

The second is
listening to the
audience

even if they aren't speaking
they will
listen back

The last is
judicious
repetition

restate the essential points
again

BLOCK

Sometimes we hit
the wall

every note
sounds false

we can't write
a decent line

new ideas
won't come

The unwavering
confidence needed
for the right solution to emerge
has departed

We can make coffee
chop wood
take a walk

each of us
has to discover
his own version of waiting

ON SUCCESS

Be grateful to your competitor
struggle with him
use all of your ethical cunning
but except in self-defense
do not try to crush him

if injured
revive him
His presence creates the pressure
to ward off
complacency

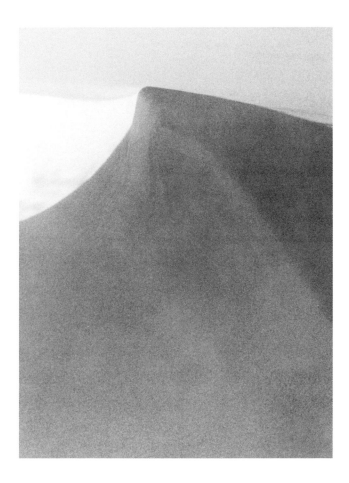

COUNTERACT

Make no mistake
it isn't all
duck and weave

Facing a belligerent adversary
sometimes you have to be willing to stand

and throw a punch

SIGNALS

The first warnings
do not come
from disturbing sirens

they come from odd displacements
and muffled voices

but these may just be the signals
of naturally changing
conditions

or false
alarms

How to keep our sensitivity
and not lose
our wits

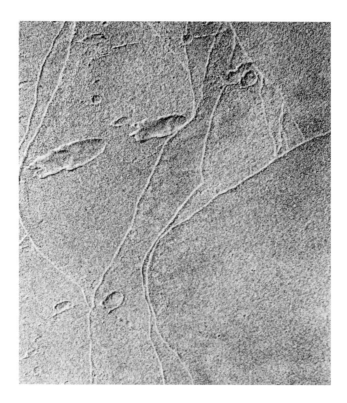

CODE OF ADDRESS

Your pontification
is almost unbearable
but even if you ask
I won't respond personally

that would pit my pontification
against yours

Hence this message
like a public key
anybody
can read

if it was meant
for you

You will decipher it
in private

DISTINCTIONS

Not doing anything
may or may not
be laziness

The visible mirrors
the invisible
which includes
the mirror

This is why what is not seen
is more fundamental
than what is

The centers of wheels
a cat asleep in realms
where mice do not go
and a monk
just sitting
are all
doing
nothing

ORGANIZATIONS

Those who think
they can do
without an organization
are deluded

Whether or not
we operate in organizations
with obviously
defined limits

we also serve in one
so great
and so extended
we hardly believe it exists

in spite of
our bumping into
tripping over
and just plain not seeing

its impressive evidence

FAILURE

After victory
failure
may be the next
best thing

In a bad performance it is easy to tell
what went wrong
In a good one
it is often hard even to find the seams

The primary lesson of failure
is to welcome being alive
then the deep learning you need
comes by itself

PRESENCE

Beauty is
the echo
that stays
after truth has sounded
its permanent harmonies

Quality is
a movement
towards the true
quietly
changing
everything

HELP

Help is the most visible and
the most mysterious factor
in the universe

The destiny of the world
depends upon
help

Hence the wider and deeper our lives
the more subtle and frequent
the help

Even the helplessness of great despair
may be a kind
of help

Bringing new weight
or cracking
something
open

UNDER EXPOSURE

Appearances
whether or not intended
to disguise

are windows
to the discerning

even a mask
can reveal a face

When the favorable moment
to be seen
suddenly arrives

be ready as best you can
to change

into
yourself

BASICS

In the business
of life
of all that we give

even in small
things

nothing is
more valuable than
our word

LESSON ONE

It is useful to know
one's own strengths
and weaknesses

but can we really
tell the difference
and by what scale do we measure

It is better to begin by knowing
that one doesn't know
oneself

than to begin
by inventing
distinctions

ADVISORS

Every leader has advisors

Some collect
subordinates whose advice
they discount
in favor of
their own

Others seek
the input of experts
in domains
where they
are lacking

The former
have hard lessons
in front of them
and will have to give
something up

The latter
will save
much time
having learned their lessons
on the way

ALL WE HAVE

To truly master it
is a rare achievement

To better apportion the lot
that is ours
is a primary struggle

On it depends sorrow
joy
possibilities

It is our most
precious
possession

the time
of our lives

MISTAKES

The wise
learn from the past

The unwise
learn from the future

The fool
learns from the future again
and again

SENSITIVITY

Letting someone go
should be done concisely
yet with the greatest care

The worst thing for both
is to wait too long

The second worst thing
is to act prematurely
without good evidence

Otherwise certain problems of yours
may never surface

HOW TO FLY

Some processes
are unfathomable
their true height
and depth
unknown to us

yet there exist
accessible intermediaries

If we invite them in
offer them
the right grain
and possess
the right temper

we may ride on their wings

STAYING ALERT

If we don't expect
the unexpected
all of our projects are at risk

Preparing for emergencies
is crucial
but not the message here

Like a rabbit in the grass

the practice suggested is
being alert
to small surprises

in front of our eyes
around our ears
under our noses

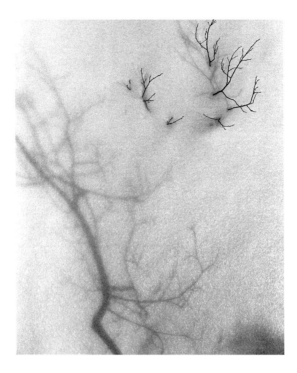

SHADOWS

Those who say that shadows are
unreal
do not know
there is a language of shadows

The wise recognize them as
messengers
that reveal
what is illuminated behind the scenes

just as certain predicaments may
convey
more knowledge
than their ultimate resolutions

WHAT IS HERE

To love what you do
resolves a hundred problems
even folding a towel
or stacking wood

the more attentive you are
the more possible this is

the less in the way
and the more room
for the fullness
of what is here

MEETINGS

Meetings
are intersections

vertices where new notions appear
where vectors of high energy
get redirected

But too many meetings
improperly conceived
under-organized
(or over-organized)

mean loss of passion
laziness and
ultimately

a boring
failure

THE MEETING

When scheduled for a session
with persons of power
visualize the situation
without flinching

consider what you're up against
if not the worst case
the second worst

then imagine
realistically
the best possible outcome

prepare for everything
if possible even
where you sit

expect surprises
unpleasant
or pleasant

they may be
opportunities

BARRIERS

One barrier
is pride
"Things must happen the way
I want them to happen"

One barrier
is dreams
"Things will happen the way
I hope they will happen"
(Success is
just around the corner)

One barrier
is stubbornness
that masquerades
as integrity

COUNTERPARTS

A person who always
counts pennies
may avoid grand failure

but is often
denied
great success

The person who never
counts pennies
may achieve great success

but is often
in grave danger
and doesn't know it

NEW MATH

Just keeping track
is integral
to a measured success
easy for person A
but impossible for person B

so given B
find A
this is elementary

an advanced course begins
with limits
that can help reveal a path
to the root of
oneself

COMMITTEES

Almost nothing major happens
unless it is processed
by a committee

committees are as inevitable
as the ripples
from an impact

nothing wrong with committees
if they occupy
their place

nowadays it's often assumed that
almost nothing major happens
unless a committee

cobbled it together
jockeyed it into shape
and punted it over our heads

Yet the singular
"almost nothings"
may make all the difference

and from them
almost everything significant
comes

CHANGE

Change is a law of nature

if you fail to adapt swiftly
you will be
sloughed off

Nevertheless

the ability
to discriminate
what doesn't change

takes precedence

CRAZY LEADERS

Some leaders may pretend
to be crazy

but some leaders
really are crazy

their finer discrimination
under the sway

of whatever craziness
has captivated them

Unless you don't mind doing something
you'd rather not

the best advice is
to stay out of their way

the smaller you are
the better

LEARNING

To learn means
to realize
something new

Yet how often
do we squint into the unknown
through the glare of knowledge

instead of searching
with a beam
of ignorance

Learning never stops
if it does
you're finished

GROUP THEORY

If you are concerned that a person of influence
will obstruct
your critical plan

put her on the task force

no matter how long a triangle
circles about its center
the order of the sides

doesn't change

But influenced by the force of the committee
working together
one might naturally

turn over

then the new circulation
will advance
everyone

FILLING A SIGNIFICANT POSITION

No one has failed
at least once
to tumble into the pit

making mistakes
is an acknowledged part
of the process

making the same one twice
suggests a reexamination
of your criteria

three times
suggests a reexamination
of yourself

PUTTING OFF

When there's a lengthy job
it is good practice
to take
everything
as it comes

the habit of
avoiding the immediate
eventually expands
minutes
hours
days

in the end
our most important endeavors
disappear
by
default

For the procrastinator
there's always
tomorrow
but

tomorrow
never
arrives

TO BE SERIOUS

One needs to be
relaxed

perhaps we can be helped
by falling in love
creating a garden
or conversing with animals

when it comes to seriousness
the grim the zealous the rigid
may be obliged to realize
that something deeper

and more wonderful
is at stake

PROMOTION

One who manages
to keep good advisors
with whom she is
comfortable
is a person of ability

One who manages
to keep good advisors
with whom she is
decidedly uncomfortable
is a person of superior ability

Advance the latter

COMPLIMENTS

The effect
of a compliment

depends upon who
bestows it

some deliver
worthy gifts

others routinely scatter
packaging material

STRESS

If we are content with
where things are headed
avoiding stress
may be intelligent

If we are uneasy about
where things are headed
escaping from our uneasiness
may be counter-productive

Consider the possibility that
within limits
there are conditions indispensable
for growth and change

this temporary discomfort
is a law
of life

UNDOING

True wonderment
is not accompanied
by exclamations

more spacious than an affirmation
more invisible than a whisper
like moving through a boundary

of a boundary

for us it begins
as a kind of lack
the sudden absence of the unreal

blocking our view

OVATION AND INNOVATION

If you seek primarily praise
you won't obtain
the truth

you may not care

If you seek primarily truth
you may not receive
the praise

you won't crumple

In spite of appearances
these two are not peers

This is an ineradicable truth
ingrained in reality

ON DIMENSION

To negotiate
takes three elements
A
B
and A times B

Not the average
because real negotiation
doesn't feel like
compromise

The best outcomes
satisfy the balance sheets
but take their shape

in regions inaccessible
to sums

A GEOMETRY OF POINTING

A finger points to the moon
but the finger
is not the moon

so pointing to the finger
is helpful only if one remembers
that the finger isn't going anywhere

otherwise
pointing to the finger that points to the moon
is simply pointing

in the wrong direction

DELEGATION

Those who cannot delegate
will invariably
cap their success
prematurely

but this may be
the better personal choice

unless the enterprise
is so top-heavy
it
sinks

CRISIS

Every series of events
worth its salt
contains a crisis

When it comes
don't indulge
in rash thinking

this is not the time
to discard years
of sober experience

But don't stand
on ceremony

act speedily
without panic

TESTING

Even if an archangel
whispered the plans
and a thousand experts
labored brilliantly
to produce a marvel

testing is obligatory

Should you doubt this
consider that we ourselves are
put to the test
in one form
or another

again and again

ENERGY

If you invest wisely
you almost always
get a fair return

If you spend
energy
knowingly

you get back
whatever you need
for the next step

OPEN SECRETS

The history of the world
is the history of secrets
coming to
light

Yet the most important secrets
are so far from us
we are unaware even of their existence
and their traces
are of no concern

Perhaps
in some other time and place
we may become invisible enough
to be able to read them
and take them to heart

like a child
grown
up

ITINERARY

The journey toward understanding
sometimes leads
through great complexity

At the heart of this complexity
is a great simplicity

obvious once recognized
yet eternally
subtle

It is the most advanced
destination

TRANSITIONS

If you wish to turn over your charge
to another

unless you are certain
it is better to assume nothing
about what they may or may not have acquired

under
your direction

In such cases
it is superior to send
the designated successor

back to study
page one

DEADLINES

In a perfect world
you might think
that deadlines would be
unnecessary

that this coercion
is needed only
to overcome our unrighteous
inertia

But this inertia
happens to be
an attribute of everything that
is

So even if
the call to action
or the desire for gain is
strong

the wise
welcome deadlines
and their quickening
force

134

TRAVELING LIGHT

Everyone can feel
the relief
of traveling light

but few of us
achieve it

Transitions
are the best time
to reduce the inventory

once settled
possessions gain power

TO BE JUST

When a responsible leader
looks through the window
of his future

he sees also the raised blind
and the delicate string
whose tug is always imminent

Thus his sight is keen
his decisions sober
and his heart glad

just to be a part
of a great
adventure

just to be

BOB SCHER served from 1995 to 2000 as president and chairman of a major computer-industry consortium. He was re-elected each year in part because he was able to unite competitors in a spirit of cooperation. Under his leadership, the organization grew from eight to over 80 corporate members, including IBM, Hewlett-Packard, and Chase Manhattan Bank. He is currently CEO of BoldElephant, Inc., a startup in online adaptive learning. Before entering the computer industry, he scripted and directed award-winning documentary films, one of which is in the permanent collection of three international film museums, including La Cinémathèque Française and The Museum of Modern Art. He is the author of *The Little Know-How Book*, *The Fear of Cooking* and articles in *Parabola*, *JAMA*, and *The American Mathematical Monthly*. He lives in Mill Valley, California. *www.bobscher.com*

JANE ENGLISH presents in her photography a unique view of the natural world. Her penetrating vision was an essential contribution to the distinguished translation by Gia-Fu Feng of the *Tao Te Ching* that brought this work to the widest English-speaking audience in history. In 1985, she founded her own publishing company, Earth Heart. As an author and photographer, her books include *A Different Doorway: Adventures of a Cesarean Born* and *Finger Pointing to the Moon*, as well as the *Mount Shasta* calendar and the evocative *Tao Te Ching* calendar. She received her doctorate from the University of Wisconsin in high-energy particle physics and is an accomplished balloonist. She lives in the small town of Calais near Montpelier, Vermont. *www.eheart.com*

INDEX